South Africa

Zoë Dawson

A ZOË BOOK

A ZOË BOOK

Original text © 1995 Zoë Dawson
© 1995 Zoë Books Limited

Devised and produced by
Zoë Books Limited
15 Worthy Lane
Winchester
Hampshire SO23 7AB
England

First published in Great Britain in 1995 by
Zoë Books Limited
15 Worthy Lane
Winchester
Hampshire SO23 7AB

A record of the CIP data is available from the British Library.

ISBN 1 874488 53 3

Printed in Italy by Grafedit SpA
Editor: Kath Davies
Design: Jan Sterling, Sterling Associates
Map: Gecko Limited
Production: Grahame Griffiths

Photographic acknowledgments

The publishers wish to acknowledge, with thanks, the following photographic sources:

The Hutchison Library / Ingrid Hudson - title page; / Liba Taylor 10; / Robert Aberman 26; Robert Harding Picture Library / J.Lightfoot 18; Impact Photos / Caroline Salguero - cover bl, 28; / Rhonda Klevansky 20; / Gideon Mendel 22; / Piers Cavendish 24; Zefa - cover tl & r, 6, 8, 12, 14, 16.

The publishers have made every effort to trace the copyright holders, but if they have inadvertently overlooked any, they will be pleased to make the necessary arrangement at the first opportunity.

Contents

All the words that appear in **bold** are explained in the Glossary on page 30.

A big map of South Africa
and a small map of the world

Dear Lucy,

You can see South Africa in red on the small map. It is a long way from home. South Africa is a big country. It is more than four times bigger than Britain.

Love,

Sara

P.S. Dad says that far fewer people live in South Africa than in Britain. About half the people in South Africa live in towns and cities.

The city of Cape Town below
Table Mountain

Dear Juba,

We are in Cape Town. It is one of the three **capital** cities of South Africa. The plane took more than 11 hours to fly here from London. We saw the African coast and the Atlantic Ocean from the plane.

Your friend,

Darren

P.S. Cape Town is on the coast. Dad says the **cape** is called the Cape of Good Hope. Table Mountain has a flat top, like a table.

A street market in Johannesburg

Dear Philippa,

Johannesburg is the biggest city in South Africa. We went shopping here. Dad gave us some South African money called *rand*. Most people here speak English. Some people speak Afrikaans.

Love,

Ginny

P.S. Mum says that Dutch people settled here long ago. Afrikaans comes from Dutch. **Native** peoples in South Africa speak many different languages.

A market stall selling fresh fruit
and vegetables

Dear Marianne,

I love the food in South Africa. We went out to lunch today. I had a huge seafood salad. We buy fresh fruit from the market every day. I like the grapes best!

Your friend,

Louisa

P.S. Dad says that South Africa sells its food all over the world. Some fish, fruit and vegetables are canned. They are loaded on to ships at Cape Town and Durban.

The Blue Train

Dear Chris,

Many people here travel by train every day. They go to work in the cities. They are called **commuters**. The Blue Train is a famous train.
I would love to travel on it.
We go by plane from city to city.

Yours,

Tommy

P.S. Dad says that there are gold mines in South Africa. Heavy goods travel by rail. There are good roads as well.

The Gemsbok National Park,
Kalahari, South Africa

Dear Annie,

We are close to the border with a country called Botswana. This park is on the edge of the Kalahari Desert. The wild animals are **protected** here. I have not seen a lion yet!

Love,

Rod

P.S. Mum says that South Africa has more kinds of wild flowers than the whole of Europe. There are many different birds as well.

An Ndebele woman making bead
jewellery, Transvaal

Dear Tina,

The Ndebele people live here in the Transvaal. The women make brightly coloured clothes like these. They also make beautiful jewellery from tiny beads.

Love,

Kate

P.S. Dad says that the Transvaal is one of the **provinces** in South Africa. Many Dutch farmers called the Boers came to live here more than 150 years ago.

In the Drakensberg Mountains

Dear Liam,

These are the highest mountains in South Africa. We have come here to see the cave paintings. They were made by the San people thousands of years ago.

Yours,

Pat

P.S. Mum says that the highest mountain in South Africa is called Mont aux Sources. It is more than 3,000 metres high.

At school in Durban

Dear Ray,

We went to school today! The children work hard. They are very quiet in the classroom. Our friend Lewis played in a football match for the school in the afternoon.

See you soon,

Lee

P.S. The teacher said that part of South Africa is in the **tropics**. The weather here is hot and damp. Farmers can grow all kinds of **crops**.

On the beach at Durban

Dear Rosie,

We have been swimming for most of the day. It is too hot to sit on the beach for long. Many people come here for holidays. Durban is one of the biggest cities in South Africa.

Love,

Annalise

P.S. Durban is on the east coast. Dad says that we have been swimming in the Indian Ocean. The **harbour** is full of big ships which take goods from Africa all over the world.

A rugby match in the Cape Province

Dear Daniel,

People play many different sports here. We have seen sports grounds in every town. Most of my friends play football every day. South Africans are very good at rugby and cricket as well.

Yours,

Ollie

P.S. Mum says that some people work all the time. They are too poor to take holidays. They sometimes play sports after work.

Carnival in Cape Town

Dear Sasha,

We have been to a **carnival** like this one today. We heard some great music. People dress up to dance and sing at **festivals** all over South Africa.

Love,

Terry

P.S. Mum says that the biggest festival was held when all the people were free to choose the rulers of the country. South Africa became a **democracy** in 1994.

The new South African flag

Dear Ali,

This is the new South African flag. Some of the colours come from the old flag. It was flown when only white people ruled the country. Other colours come from the flag black people flew at that time.

Love,

Jonas

P.S. Dad says the leaders who rule the country meet in Cape Town. The other capital cities are Pretoria and Bloemfontein.

Glossary

Cape: A piece of land which sticks out into the sea.

Capital: The town or city where people who rule the country meet.

Carnival: A special time when people dress up in costumes. They dance in the streets.

Commuter: Someone who travels some distance to and from work each day.

Crops: Plants that farmers grow.

Democracy: A country where all the people choose the leaders they want to run the country.

Festival: A time when people remember something special that happened in the past. People often dance and sing during a festival.

Harbour: A place where ships can shelter.

Native: Someone who was born in the place or country where they live.

Protect: To look after. People are not allowed to pick wild plants or to hunt wild animals in National Parks. The wildlife is protected so that it does not die out.

Province: Part of a country which is like a county or a state. People who run a province are chosen by the people who live in it.

P.S.: This stands for Post Script. A postscript is the part of a card or letter which is added at the end, after the person has signed it.

Tropics: The lands near the middle of the Earth. The heat from the Sun is strongest here. We draw lines on maps to show the position of the tropics.

Index